SONGS OF THE MONADNOCKS

Songs of the Monadnocks

Selected Poems

Gwendolyn Eisenmann

ELDER MOUNTAIN PRESS

Songs of the Monadnocks
Copyright © 1999 by Gwendolyn Eisenmann

Published by Elder Mountain Press

All rights reserved.
No part of this book may be used or reproduced
in any form whatsoever without written permission
from the author and publisher.

Typeset, printed and bound in the United States of America
Printer and bindery: Thomson-Shore, Inc.

Library of Congress Catalog Card Number 99-066471
ISBN 0-9668075-2-9

Elder Mountain Press
PO Box 1256
West Plains, MO 65775

For information and orders of additional copies, please contact Elder Mountain Press at the above address.

Cover: the Monadnocks from Caney Mountain, in Ozark County, Missouri. Photograph by Marideth Sisco
Design by Susie Nightowl

Introduction

Gwendolyn Eisenmann and husband Art decided to retire in the Ozarks after traveling here to visit a son who had moved here. While touring the area, they turned west on a highway in Ozark County, drove over a hilltop, and had their first view of the Gainesville Monadnocks.

The word "monadnock" is believed to be of Native American origin, and means "hill that stands alone." Monadnocks are formed by erosion of a high plateau whose upper layer of rock is very hard. This creates an area of deep valleys and steep slopes that hosts a wild and varied habitat. It was here, in the era of market hunting, that the state's last wild turkey flocks were found amid the cane thickets and spring-fed hollows. Gwen knew nothing of this. She only knew that when she saw the Monadnocks, she had come home.

Once here, she found herself returning to an early dream, unrealizable in the Depression. Then, when money was scarce, she studied nursing. It became her career for 27 years. Once in the Ozarks, she revisited her first love. She returned to college at age 73 and in 1996 completed a Master of Arts degree in Personal Essays and Poetry.

The poems in this volume offer eloquent expressions of ideas, visions and the mute language of the senses; senses born of listening in the evening quiet and the bird-filled mornings, to the songs and voices of this unlikely paradise. Gwen pens the verses; a husband, three children and four grandchildren lead the chorus of voices in this compelling work.

July 1999, Marideth Sisco, Elder Mountain Press

Contents

Chorus

Chorus 1
Daybreak 2
Housewarming 3
Three 4
Where in the world— 6
Family reunion 7
For her ninetieth birthday 8
Sonnet for Marion 10
Marion's baptism 11
Marion catches stars 12
Baptism 13
Wedding anniversary 14
Gretchen 15
Grandchild 16
Gathering eggs with Heather 17
You just have to love them 18
Fishing 20
My father 21
He's 80 and leaning into it 22
One Morning 23

Remembering

Michaelmas 27
Remembering 28
November day 29
February 30
Arrival of spring 31
Little lake at evening 32
April Rain 33
Untitled 34

Parenthesis

Transplant   37
Parenthesis   40
Picture a garden   41
Annular eclipse of the sun   42
Bee alive   43
Bees   44
Garden in a clearing   45
Three gardeners   46
Sunday morning   47
Idyll   48
Homing   49
Worm psalm   50
Corn silk   51
Fall garden   52
Ripe pears   53
Meadow   54

Sunglasses

Legacy   57
Old house   58
Doors   59
Crop Circles   60
Metaphor   61
After cataract surgery   62
Question   63
Life is a lonely place   64
Just before sleep   65
Dead cardinal   66
Hospital city   67
Sunglasses   68
Reflection   69

*For my family and my friends,
who composed the score for the lyrics.*

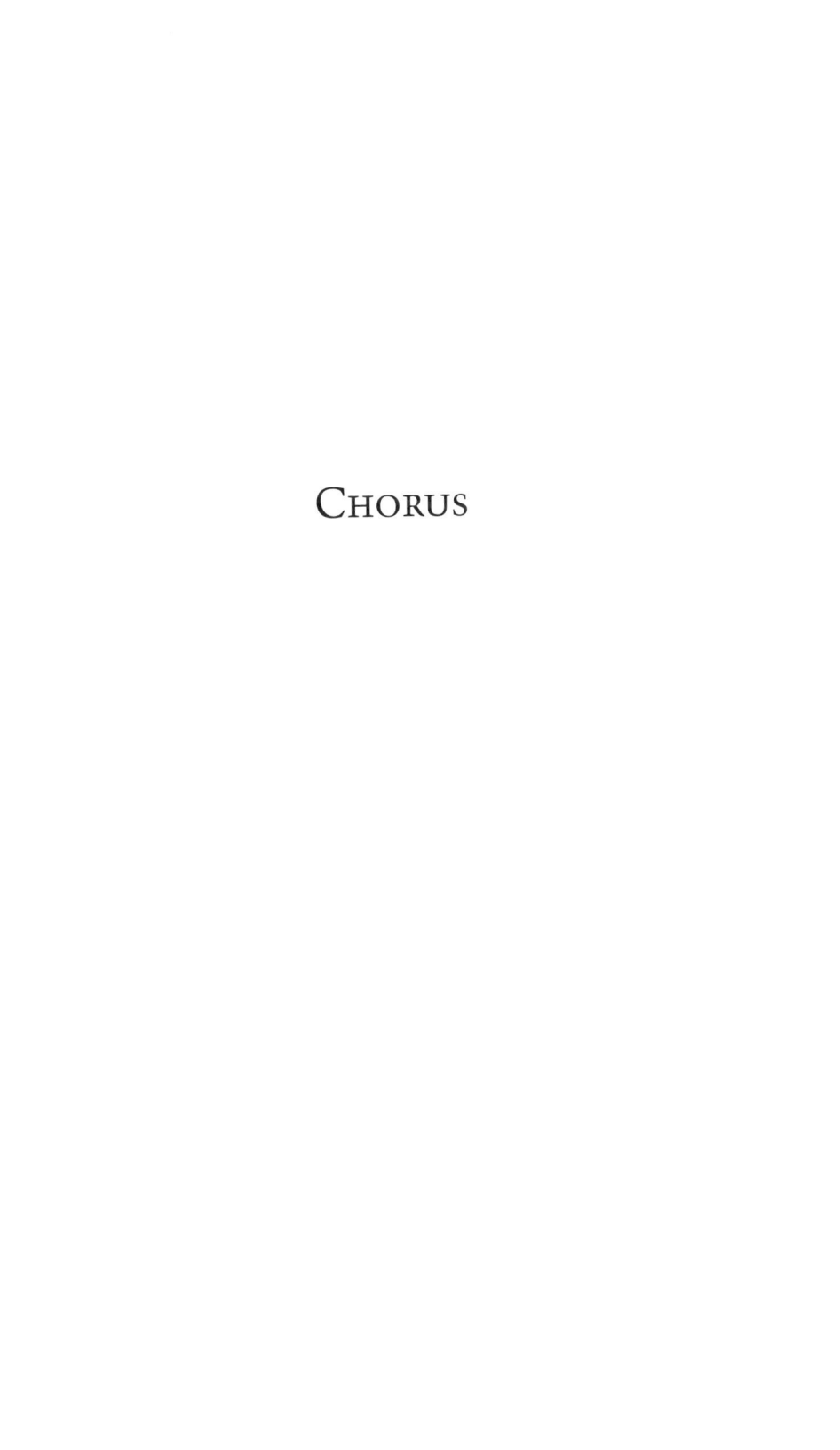

Chorus

Chorus

"I can't hear myself think,"
Mother used to say
when we were noisy children.
It wasn't the thoughts so much
as the loss of self to think them.
Now, alone, walking a woodsy lane
at dusk, everything stilled but katydids,
hearing myself think, the sounds
are all of others, the parts of me
that they have become.

Daybreak

Rain whispers me awake. A mourning dove
toots its mellow flute as morning sings
of things too tender to endure the love
of sun and heat in high July. The wings
I hear asweep the eaves will cover nests
to shelter nestlings new to sun and rain;
and I will tender, too, my love who rests
and dreams the sibilant sound of rain's refrain.
Before I leave this mystic hour of dawn,
before the mist disperses into light,
before I hear the day astir upon
the silence of the house, before the bright
of new-washed sun turns everything to gold,
imprinted is this hour of joy I hold.

Housewarming

Come in! There is a welcome waiting here
that grew, as did the house, in winter sun
and rain, with wishes for a shelter near
old friends, old longings long ago begun.
A house up high uplifts the traveler's eye
and gives a view o'er which a spirit soars
to see the Earth around. The eagle's cry
will mingle with intent within these doors.
We build our sanctuaries all enclosed
but space enclosed is room for resonance
where souls can shout, where secrets here disclosed
can harmonize our human dissonance.
    The blessing in the welcome here today
    is what we bring and what we take away.

Three

I know it is true because
in my soul it reverberates,
brings back the prayer
my mother prayed before I was born.

A woodthrush's song at dawn,
the call of wild geese in flight,
Christmas snow, summer thunder
are her voice.

I was only three, but I remember
apple fritters for breakfast.
Mother put one on my plate
and I broke off little crispy tailings
and crunched them, one by one.

Dad was going to Grandma's house.
I had to choose to go
or to stay and eat my fritter.
Dad wrapped it in a napkin
for me, and I walked beside him
down the street past the firehouse
where the firemen waved at me.

Mother held me on her lap.
We sat on the floor.
She gave me a spoonful of cod liver oil

on the promise of an orange to suck.
We shared an orange cut in half,
sucking the wonderful juice
that Dad said made my hair curly.

My sister was older.
We had a baby brother
when I was not quite three.
My sister and I were sent
to a neighbor's to play.
The bigger girls put me in a baby carriage
and pushed me down the street.
Dad came out on our porch to call
"come see your baby brother."

He was very small in the crib
beside Mother's bed.
I looked at him
then climbed onto the big bed
to be closer to Mother.
A few months later she was gone.

Where in the world—

Where in the world do I belong? Where
Am I not on hold? What other place
Feels like my garden, yet allows a face
To float among the flowers, and to care?
Who understands transplanting? Who's aware
Of sun that slants, and shadows that displace
The sense of being in a certain space?
In a cocoon I move from here to there.
Who and where would make me feel at home?
The scattered bits of soul I've left behind
Must make a pattern. Everywhere I roam
Someone creates an essence. When I find
A formula for mine, how sweet the loam
Fresh-planted, with its fragrance thus defined!

Family Reunion

The familiar braided years
of dark and light
that bind us together
have patterns that repeat
and we came to examine this tapestry again.

There is a lustre
where holes were pinned
with stars to mark
where figures were complete
and colors made a signature.

Black where a jagged storm
tore the cloth to shreds
but the warp remained
and children gathered up the threads
to mend with an orange woof of joy.

Yellow for summer, blue for distance,
red for holiday, and silver gray
to soften texture rough with learning.
Feel the thickness where
small knots were tied,

one thread becomes two, then three or more;
and here where missing threads
are caught up again,
how warm the fabric, how strong.
Enough for a cloak for each of us.

For Her Ninetieth Birthday

What do you bring to someone who is ninety?
Another day?

The eagle rides the valley wind
low, between the hills
where the sun lights rocks
as white as his tail.
I stand above him.
Who would dream of standing
higher than the eagle?

A mammoth sycamore is down
that leaned across the slough,
white branches spread like fingers
on the other bank,
wide roots tipped up, way up above my head.
Who would dream of standing
beneath the roots of the sycamore?

The rock cove is curtained
where a spring drips icy lace,
but down below the pool still shimmers
where a deer drank
and left a two-toed print at the edge.
Suddenly the sun with dazzling fingers
touches the ice.
Who would dream of standing
where morning is made?

Wood wind, running water,
golden seal, blue mushrooms,
smell of oak and age, and mystery.
Who would dream of standing
where ninety years is young?
Whose cup is carved so deep
it no longer overflows with wonder?

What do you bring to someone who is ninety?
Another day?

Sonnet for Marion

What could be lovelier than baby girls?
A bud, a bloom, a butterfly, a bird?
A bud has yet to be; a bloom unfurls
then fades, its fragrance gone, its beauty blurred.
Ah, butterfly, your wings with Angel dust
soft shimmering in golden summer light
are beautiful, but still their fanning must
give way to breath of baby girls at night.
The feathers of a bird, its flight, its song
are fashioned more of Heaven than of Earth,
so wonder might the most to them belong
except for cheeks of baby girls at birth.
    How do I know the loveliest to love?
    This baby Marion does all this prove.

Marion's Baptism

Her father asked, "shouldn't we have a priest?"
"You are a priest," her mother replied.
They went to the river on her fortieth day,
    (Forty days it rained, the Jews wandered,
    Jesus fasted, Buddha sat beneath the Bodhi tree)
where her father Priest dipped his finger
to trace a triangle on her brow.
By her name she was consecrated
to the Holy Trinity
and blessed by her mother
for the thoughts that will be hers.
"Marion Luce, Light of the Virgin, is your name."

They went to the garden on her fortieth day
where her father Priest dipped his finger
in salt, crystalline symbol of earth,
to trace a square on her chin.
Once again the consecration,
once again her mother's blessing
for the will that is hers.

They went to the hilltop on her fortieth day,
to the house that holds their lives,
where her father dipped his finger
in ash of a cedar tree
to trace a cross on her heart.

Name, consecration, blessing
that her feelings may be
always loving, encompassing all.
They stood there in the sun on her fortieth day
and prayed the Lord's Prayer, and cradled their child.

Marion Catches Stars

Marion catches stars
when she goes out at night.
So recently come from
their realm she's at home
in their midst. Holding up
cupped hands to the sky
she brings me her treasure, reverently.
I take it, hold it, then give it back.
She kisses it, hands still cupped deep,
and tosses it high again.

It's simple. I should have
thought of it before.
Mysterious and far, I didn't realize
stars come to those who hold up their hands.
Stars are. Marion knows that.

Baptism

About as tall as the table
under which she plays
with a hand-held mirror,
rapt in the gaze

of herself, she knows
the mysterious Other
but hasn't words
to tell what she knows.

"Me," she says, and runs away.
But later that day, down at the creek,
splashing, learning to duck her head,
she did it, came up laughing and said,

"I got it!" The Other was born.

Wedding Anniversary

The best relationships can't be explained
but they endure because of alchemy.
I love you not for what was thus obtained,
but for the golden days of mystery
that held us close, when all that then remained
to reach the ultimate, the final key,
was just to write it down, and be champagned
for thus achieving immortality.

We never wrote it down, it slipped away.
The transmutation happened anyhow
and aging gave its own unique bouquet.
Whatever "it" was doesn't matter now.
There is no recipe for time but this:
always throw out the last analysis.

Gretchen

She was sophisticated, a personnel director
who knew how to manipulate, impress, get
attention. Petite, sexy, dark
with black curly hair I so admired,
she was like a siren, beckoning
to me, a puppy eager for her hand
to lift me up to taste what she ate.
She made me feel I was something I was not.

It wasn't comfortable wearing a friend
that didn't fit. Though it was her idea
that we be friends, I was flattered
thinking she liked the contrast in me.
She was the flower, I was the bee
but the nectar was bitter, the fragrance heavy
with exotic unknowns, pervading and toxic,
overcoming my hesitancy.

It was like driving while intoxicated.
I crashed, her enticements evaporated
like wine gone flat. Back in my own garden
I sipped simple things: dandelions and dew.

Grandchild

Three score and ten, they say,
is the sum of living.

But mortality, wistfully,
becomes immortality vividly.

Suddenly this bud of a baby
brings remembrance, continuance.

We go side by side, stepping
in and out of earthly life,

the older sheltering the younger,
then reverse our rolls.

Gathering Eggs with Heather

It's raining a bit
so we'll take an umbrella.
Heather is three
and holds the umbrella high.

Jake, head rooster,
signals the hens
with a guttural squawk.
Dim light in the coop,
we pause and look.
Though the door is open
hens linger inside
out of the rain, singing.

We walk softly on the straw,
Heather picks up a fluffy feather,
forgotten the eggs
in the wonder of her find.

I lift her to look in a nest
to see what we can see.
Two eggs!
One, as warm and brown as her hand,
she holds and gives me the feather.
Umbrella, eggs and feather,
Heather and I walk out in the rain.

You just have to love them

You just have to love them—
people, that is,
when you learn how ingenious
they've been to survive
and stay sane, and love,
after what they've been through,
more, to enjoy being alive.

It seems odd to me–
the choices we have,
they call it free will
but it's really not free;
there's always a price
though we name it ourselves.
We pay what we choose to be.

Whatever the choice
we somehow conform
and shape the results
to fit our own schemes,
paying our dues
somehow or other,
composing original themes.

You just have to love them
because it is
yourself you see

in their genius, their quest
to answer the question
of how to survive.
The answer: to love yourself first.

Consider loving
this gift of self,
this perfect model
of spirit; adore
this "I", God-given
along with the trust
to know who you are, and what for.

Fishing

Streamside. Sunny morning in May.
Trout eager for bait,
Laughter of men and women on holiday.

A snake glides by, nose up,
hardly different from a leaf or two.
Indifferent snake. No one notices.

I saw a mink, black, sleek,
blacker than the shadows it silently threads
where no one notices.

Rock cliff, quiet water sliding
by indifferent people
fishing for each other.

My Father

My father,
         who art now in Heaven,
smelled of witch hazel shaving lotion.

His beard and hair were black,
         his chin strong, with a deep dimple,
his shoulders were wide and square. His shirts
were always starched and ironed smooth,
white, with white duck pants sharp creased
he wore for holidays, picnics, parades.

I longed to have him hug me,
to be close, to talk of private things,
to tell me of my mother
who died when I was three.
But he couldn't.
He wasn't strong enough
to cry with me.
Men didn't do that.

He wanted me to be
his baby daughter forever,
or, if grown,
the epitome of womanhood.
But I couldn't.
I wasn't strong enough.
He forgot to tell me how,
and couldn't cry with me.
Men didn't do that.

My father, who art now in Heaven,
I still love you.
Your dignity still wears starched shirts.

He's 80, and Leaning Into It

He walks with a staff, feet wide apart
for balance, rocking from side to side,
stepping heavily, bent a little
from the hips, gathering momentum
trying to catch his own forward lean
and, instead, almost falling on his face,
stopping, to start the gait over again
on legs that once jumped from combat planes.

But this morning, loving him so, I reached
for a hug, and got it, strong and warm
from the heart, the shoulders, head and torso,
the great heart of him engulfing me.
A thick rubber mat on the floor where we stood
in our embrace unbalanced him
as he stepped back, but the great heart
never stumbled, never will.

Those arms, those hands that milked the cows,
split wood, carved bowls and spoons, built barns,
drove horses, husked corn,
carried children as they slept,
are still as strong as love can be.

One Morning

He was fishing,
fly rod flicking
feathers to a shadow
near the opposite bank.

Strike! a rainbow
leaped and shone in sunlight,
moment exquisite,
rod bent, line tight.

Netted, landed, hand trembling
from the thrill,
old man young as
      the rhythm of the river,
feet wide apart
      against the current
of all the years rushing by.

Timeless, the river, the fish, the man
swaying together
to a cosmic plan
      of promise in rainbows.

Remembering

Michaelmas

Rush of summer is over.
Earth and I draw our shawls close
and watch evening glow come early.
One star - or maybe a spark
from Michael's sword
hung there in crystal.

Light the fire, Papa,
dreams are coming,
pictures stored in summer sun,
still warm with color.
Things to cherish, seeds to keep,
dried blossoms still fragrant,
memories that somehow become inspiration.

I'll start new compost tomorrow
with spent roses to add: sublime potpourri.
Inspiration becomes creation.

But summer's rush is over,
Earth and I hug ourselves
'round the life we've stored.
Creation becomes meditation.

Remembering

Here by the edge of October
where the sun leans left
and the hill tilts up
I saw geese flying
      to an old compelling
           calling calling calling.

There at the tip of November
where the moon is full
and coyotes sing
I saw trees shiver
      remembering leaves
           falling falling falling.

November Day

Hilltop
pines comb the wind
catching sound. One oak leaf
dances down the valley
where it opens into blue.
A small child says
"Look at that leaf!"
and dances too.

February

Rain. A small word
of great significance,
a fourth of life's definition,
mood watercolor.

I've worn out February.
The last chapter of winter
has tattered pages of thought.
One last word, "rain,"
dimples puddles of sighs
before catalogs close
on warm jackets.

Arrival of Spring

Night comes on, and Spring, tiptoeing through the dark,
slips on an icy skate that March left lying in the park.
She spills the flower seeds that she was sowing there,
but laughs to think where they will grow, too happy, far,
to care.

All night long the rain fell softly
whispering — whispering.

The sudden brilliance of the day
awoke me, and in green array
April stood there in the sun
opening leaf buds, one by one.

Little Lake at Evening

Loud the catbirds call across the lake,
blackbirds' toneless whistles
                      o'er the water break;
white ducks, silver ribbons
                      shimmering after them,
glide to nests beneath blackberry's dipping stem.

April Rain

Sweet, sweet to wake to sound of raindrops in the
spring,
 the oriole pipes his sad accented whistle-ing
into the muted music of the rain.
Or does the rain accompany the oriole's words?
Which is the water's voice and which the bird's?

Pipe softly, Oriole, there is a distant thrush
that sends his vibrant call to echo in the hush
of early morning's quiet April rain.

Untitled

All sounds are singing;
It may be of gnomes
or dragons, or pain,
or rain, or feathers that fall
on a hornet's nest,
but all sounds are singing.

Parenthesis

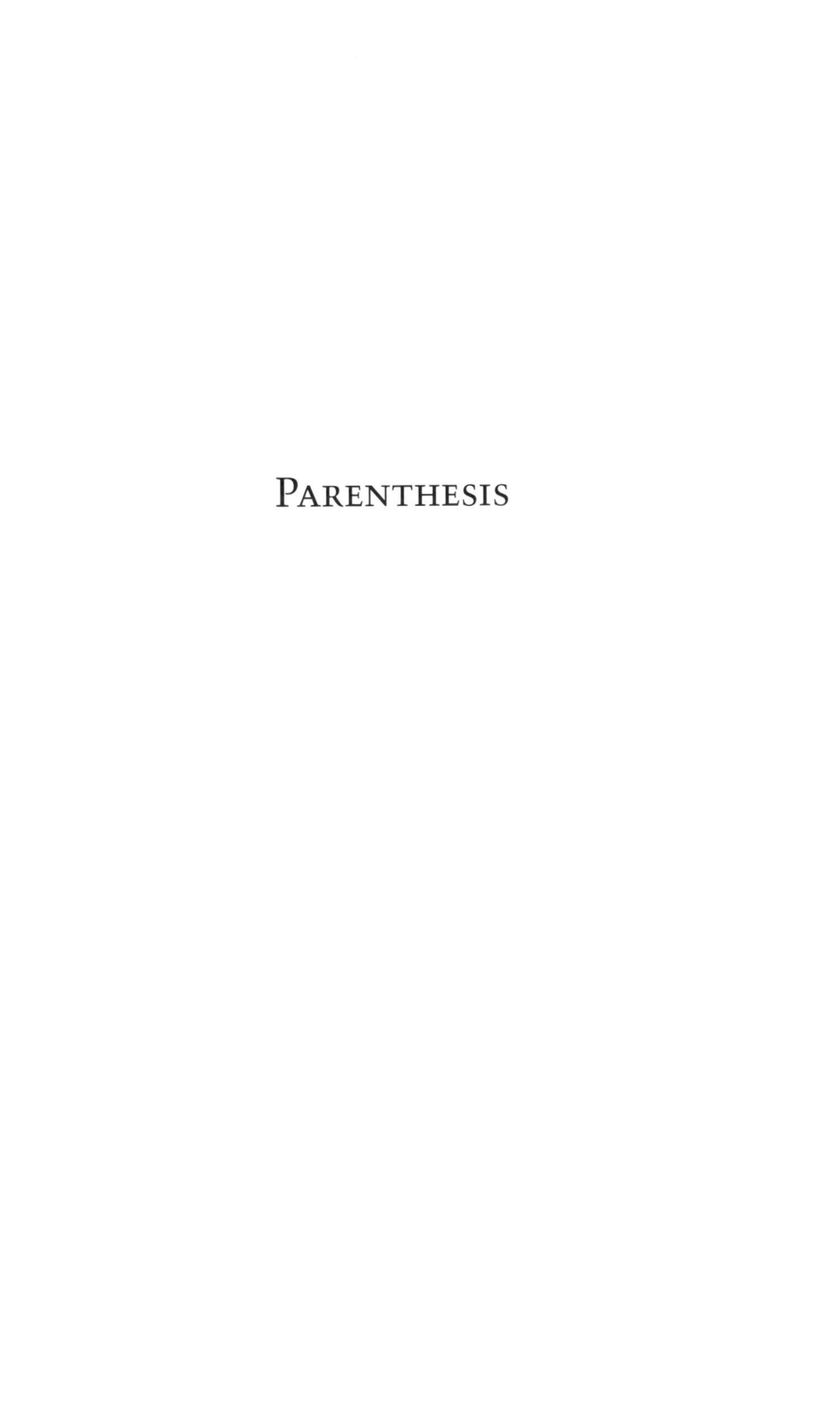

Transplant

It was a wild place
when we came to it.
We thought it was a forest
like we'd known before
friendly, benign, flowered.
We cleared the brush
and built a house.

Eagles came in winter,
and woodpeckers with red crests
and hammering bills.
We watched and waited
but we didn't belong.

Old trees sheltered us,
their wood kept us warm.
We watched and waited
through bright days and starry nights
but we didn't belong.

Spring came (it never seemed
to be really winter),
so we cleared more brush
and made a garden.
The forest towered over us, watching,
untouched by our tugging at her skirt
We wanted to love her
and for her to love us
but we didn't know her name.
We didn't belong.

Radishes grew in our garden,
and down along the river
spice bush bloomed.
Suddenly in the garden
bluebirds and robins appeared,
and verbena and violets.
They liked the clearing
and we were glad.

Seasons came and went,
the garden grew,
deer, turkeys, snakes and turtles
lived there too.
It was we who didn't belong.

Dark days came
with trouble and turmoil,
heartache and pain.
We eased the hurt in the garden
growing flowers and fruit.
The forest was impassive but peaceful.
We buried pain in the garden.

All the forest creatures gathered.
We built a fence
so we too could eat.
They didn't belong there.
Starlight and moonlight lit the clearing
and butterflies came in sun.

Mushrooms bloomed in the forest shadows,
and the forest grew around us.
It was a wild place
alive with truth.
So we stayed in our house
where we belong
and the forest shelters us.

Parenthesis

A clearing in a forest will do.
A peculiar peace settles there.
People come, and the absence
of people noise is awesome to them
or frightening, depending on who they are.

Picture a Garden

Words will not suffice but pictures will
without frames, except the weathered kind:
wind, sun, rain in August haloing the view.

But even if the garden would hold still,
if flowers did not bend
or birds rise and descend,
if bushes did not breathe butterflies;

Or bees appear and disappear
and hum and stir in blossoms
that not only take, but make light;

If trellises were only raising roses
and not enticing purple birds to perch,
If rows would stay in rows
without surprises popping up
making tapestry appear to be the plan;

If noontime did not fade into glowtime
when dusk darkens the frame
and colors glow as though they stored sunlight
for just this evening show,

Even if the garden would hold still
a frame could not contain her heart, my soul.

Annular Eclipse of the Sun

Imagine causing the Sun to dim.
Imagine being the Moon
swung in a cosmic sling
making so great a shadow
Earth holds her breath in awe.

In the garden, in that hour of rapture,
I hugged my bare arms against the chill
of silence before the Almighty.
"Be still, and know that I am God,"
said the Sun, and birds stopped singing,

trees and breeze stopped humming.
Bumblebees were all that moved,
heads buried in honey dips of blossoms
so they did not know. It felt sacrilegious to speak
while bathed in the seldom seen light of a halo.

Then on patio rocks beneath a dogwood tree
appeared a sign, a signature:
Crescent suns in perfect pattern.
"I am that I am," who paints pictures with a wash
of peach-colored light in air.

Filled with reverence for a picture so pure
the flowers and I knew each other
when high delight of bright sunlight
was filtered through the Moon
leaving only a Ring of Truth.

Bee Alive

What is a bee?
He is a she
usually.

What is a queen?
Laying machine,
soon a has been.

What is a drone?
He bee on loan
serving the throne.

What is a hive?
House of bee jive,
honey dive.

Bees

do as they please
but please to do
what pleases their queen
more or less

who hides in the dark
laying eggs
making bees
who do as they please

in a forest of flowers
and heady scent
making honey from these
with nectar they squeeze

color seduced
dance reduced
to just being bees
more or less.

Garden in a Clearing

This clearing in the forest we have made
To gentle us a place to call our own—
To look as if we could command a glade
All fenced, all planned and planted, newly grown—
Has somehow turned intention all around.
The garden has become a Being bright,
Entrancing, dancing, gay with sight and sound,
Who beckons from the forest with her light.
What new perspective purple birds can bring
To proper rows from packages! She glows
With shimmering butterflies, with birdsong sings,
And flings around her gown a scarlet rose.
    A different dawn from what I thought to see
    Awakens different flowering in me.

Three Gardeners

We sat around a table, talking late,
Three astral beings and the rest of us.
These astral beings are quite luminous
Discussing how they can communicate
With plants by gesture, color, attitude
Bold or shy, or messages they get
By tuning in with their souls' alphabet
Of feelings to the plants' serenitude.

Oh they are mortal gardeners, those three,
Though they can find their way to fairylands
And then return with stardust on their hands
To seed the soil with flower wizardry.
At least, to hear them talk, that's how it seems.
I wonder how it feels to ride moonbeams?

Sunday Morning

Christians call it the Lord's day,
first day of the week,
but the Lord rested on the seventh day
and then went on creating.

I walked the lane early
before July scorched the air.
It was cool enough to bless
and warm enough to blue the haze
where shafts of sun slanted
through small clearings in the woods.

The only visible movement was
ants in wheel tracks
hurrying somewhere, where
other ants were going.
Leaves hung still, sun and shade
fixed. A woodpecker drummed,
startled me, so close, so loud.

Small tarantula walked past, jet black and glossy,
fuzzy thick antennae pointed straight ahead.
I turned to watch
eight legs alternating
in unhurried perfect synchrony
going— where?

High bush huckleberry
underneath the old dead pine
dropped ripe berries in my hand.
Blueberry flavor with just a hint of tart
bitterness when I chewed the skin.
Greenbrier climbs the dead pine pillar.

Idyll

A garden, June, late afternoon, potluck
With neighbors (neighbors here are miles apart)
Who have been helping with the hay. I pluck
A sprig of peppermint to chew. We start
Uncovering casseroles of food; the smells
Are mingled with the peppermint and hay.
A couple, long away, return, and tell
Of leaving smoggy cities. Home to stay,
They look, and look at acres long unused
Now beds of herbs, in order and in flower.
We eat and talk. The couple, now bemused,
Are quiet in the evening garden bower.
  A little girl takes grown-ups by the hand
  To ring-around-a-rosy in the sand.

Homing

Blowing away yesterday
I followed clouds
over a hill,
past ponds and pumpkin patches
and barns and crowing roosters,
past the osage hedge
yellow in sunlight.

Past full moon
beyond frost
there was a garden
newly dressed,
patted smooth for winter,
parsley bed
still emerald green.

Oh my garden!
far away
winking out your flowers,
hold my hope for me
a little while.

Worm Psalm

O worm, (which end do I bespeak?)
thou makest not a sound nor squeak,
but I forsooth would sing thy praise
and thank thee for thy quiet ways.

Thou eatest the earth, O squiggly worm,
and spitteth it out in curdly form
to fluffeth thy bed 'round flower feet,
and aireth thy head in tunnely neat.

Thou'rt nothing but a strip and squirm,
no shape, no drape, unlovely worm,
but we without thee sure would die,
so bless the earth wherein thee lie.

Ah crumbly soil! ah humusy deeps
wherein my wormy garden keeps
a secret scent distilled by thee,
O wiggly worm, abide with me!

Corn Silk

Have you been in a cornfield,
perhaps as a child,
running down the rows
of this vast green growing
knowing giants live there
storing nuggets of gold
in fat green pouches
tied with silk?

Fall Garden

October colors melt in rain,
red runs into purple
and orange to rust.
Sky clears, and that incredible blue
borders and backdrops
forest and hills.

Garden, her face
damp and sweet
composed for sleep,
shakes seeds from her hair
nestles into a bed of straw
and folds her life within.

Round like the moon
shining like sun
smooth as wind
seeds pocket secrets.

"Do not open until"
you've made a wish.

Ripe Pears

The fragrance of ripe pears came to me
and I saw them, yellow, smooth, small urns
holding remnants of summers I remember.
I was a child at our old farmhouse
where pear trees were just outside the back door
and the ground underneath was full of ripe pears.
I was thirsty, and hungry, taking bites
and drinking juice that dribbled down my chin.
The air was warm with pear scent that drew
buzzing insects to suck the sweetness too.
Yellow jackets, yellow and brown like the pears,
and wasps and bald-faced hornets, and bees
all innocently sharing the nectar so
freely given and fearlessly chosen.
Children drinking from the breast of the mother,
unconscious bliss is what we were.

Meadow

There is a meadow in morning sun
where jeweled spider webs are hung,
dazzling trellises of light
that fairies play upon at night.

They climb, they strum where spiders sleep
knowing the watch spiders keep
is not for fairy feet and wings;
they dream of flies and juicy things.

First light becomes a meadow's blush,
she holds her breath, awaits the brush
of breeze to dry her tangled hair
and comb the spider from his lair.

The meadow is embroidered so
with lacy webs that silver glow
I wish the sun would stop at dawn
and stay and stay with morning on.

Sunglasses

Legacy

They said they'd buy our house with all its land
That we must sell because we've grown beyond
The fixing of its fences, and its grand
Design of stairways, and its garden pond.
How will we tell them of the legacy
Of love that built this house upon a hill
With heart and soul, creating sanctuary?
On second thought, I guess we never will.
The eagle will return in winter sun,
The flowers in the garden bloom anew,
The deer will come and gaze at anyone,
The hills will stay, and seasons paint the view.
      We're ready. We have had the best of it.
      We'll keep the ache, but give the rest of it.

Old House

Old House, for twenty years I thought of you as new,
still developing a personality
because we built you, with trees and rocks
from the hill, looking down the valley
where the river always is.

We went back last night, invited to dinner,
having left you three months ago (did you miss us
as we missed you?). I felt moving day
again, the feeling of stripping you, gutting you,
leaving you alone to gather up
the pieces of our lives left in your corners.

But there, as I turned my back
on my garden, my sanctuary, my soul,
there were three young women, apprentice gardeners
walking wide-eyed through the gate
and you welcomed them with the bluebird,
sprouts in the garden, warmth in your walls
and wind from the south.

Three young women asked us to dinner,
with flowers from my garden,
and I tasted wonder again, flavored with pain
of their trials, their longing to live into the silence
and the mystery of the forest around.
Oh I know, I know the comfort of your walls,
Old House, I know every stone
in your fireplace, and the women asked us

(as if we could name) the lessons we learned
while we were there. We do not want to
do it over again. They keep you scrubbed
and spare. Teach them who they are.

Doors

I went back to the old house today.
The lane through the forest looks just the same,
close and green, just a hint of September
in sassafras orange and sumac red,
veils of sunlight flung through trees,
fastened with spiderwebs, fringed with ferns.

The house is almost hidden behind
beds of tall flowers, amaranth and salvia
that lean against the garden fence.
The elder bush beside the shop
was stripped of berries, their juice
in jars on kitchen counters.

No one was home except the dog.
I started to collect bits of self
I had left behind. Cupboard doors were ajar
on hand-carved walnut hinges with hickory pegs.
I closed the doors.

Crop Circles

We don't hear much about
the hieroglyphics of grain
except in some offbeat Ag publications
or talk in the counter culture
"back-to-the-landers" still back there.

Some say there is nowhere
left on Earth to explore
except perhaps bottoms of oceans.
Every horizon has vanished.
We've been to the moon
and probed planets with pictures.

Then whose finger traces
messages in fields of grain,
circles and pathways partitioned
to lead a probing mind
through a maze, perhaps
the heart of the millenium?

Some of them look like keyholes.
Where is the key? E.T.s
and energy some say.
I'm just glad there's an alphabet
not yet deciphered.

Metaphor

I think that all the crises we endure
Are training for the greatest one of all:
The separation from what seemed so sure
When we were young, our present self. To fall
From life we hold to so tenaciously
But wake before we land, as in a dream,
And feel our cherished senses floating free
From Spirit self, with no return, must seem
The greatest crisis we will ever know,
The greatest loss. But freedom so profound—
With unadulterated love to show
The way beyond with shining all around—
The great adventure we are training for
Must make death seem a tired metaphor.

After Cataract Surgery

It was like a club meeting,
a gathering of Cyclops.
We sat in the waiting room

each with a bandage over one eye.
We'd leave with dark glasses,
having never clearly seen each other.

En masse they cut into our eyes
our brains, our lives, like an exercise
to purge us of our years.

No time to warn my eye,
to nurse its conscious wound,
to get used to being different.

The doctor was kind, sending us home
with drops and shield
in place of who we were.

I told myself, "this is
an adventure, savor it. Isn't it marvelous
what they can do?"

The marvel is my brain, eye
that sees looking out
without anyone looking in.

Question

Why is my inside so different from my outside?
I don't look to be who I really am.
Or am I really who I look to be?
Then who is the person I think I am?

Skin side? Inside? We live together
But sometimes one doesn't fit the other.
Carrying me around I wonder
Who is myself— me, or the other?

Life is a Lonely Place

Life is a lonely place—
come dance with me.

Hear the night voice
calling to the day voice
      through a hole
          in the moon
where tomorrow comes
to comfort you.

O morning!
slide a silken hue
     across a splintered
         rainbow.

Life is a lonely place—
come dance with me.

Just Before Sleep

Of my oblique that slips a slanting plane
    of selfishness across a day's good grain

I think in silence, and am glad for night
    soft-shoeing sideways making curious right.

Dead Cardinal

Everyone sees what a poet sees:
a cardinal lying dead in snow
his brilliance undiminished by death
bright wound on a somber day, aglow.

Gray sky, white snow, red bird so still
when wind and heart mourn a eulogy
and recognize what is given:
beauty frozen in memory.

Everyone hears what a poet hears
except the song of a frozen bird:
the snow, the sky, the loss, the gain,
the quivering birth of a crimson word.

Hospital City

There are domed skylights
and tall trees
in the lobby of Hospital city.
People sit on overstuffed lounges
in groups and along walls
where maroon upholstery and gray carpets
soften sound and feelings.

Space swallows resonance
where families converse in soft voices,
wheelchairs whisper past,
volunteers spend hours
recharging souls, their own
and others, with pink coats
and answers
that don't answer anything.

In the center, on a large table
covered with glass, is a model
of "Existing" and "Expansion."
Physicians' offices occupy one wing
to record and re-evaluate
why we are here.
Secrets stored there hide
our mechanical and chemical analyses
which have nothing to do
with sunlight, moonlight and starlight
through the skylights
over trees growing inside.

Sunglasses

Driving west in the afternoon
I put sunglasses on, new
amber-colored wrap-arounds.
Cloud masses, with sun behind,
became mysterious mountains with
layered canyons and heights outlined
in silver at the top, green depths below.
They were places to explore,
small worlds floating in a pale green sky.
I was awed looking at places
I had never seen before,
each one defined, softened, flowing
from senses refined, finally knowing

the Spirit of things must be like that,
not obscured by too much radiance,
showing itself in a different light
at certain times, in certain places.

On "Found Poems" from the *Annie Dillard Reader, a collection.*

Reflection

Annie Dillard found poems
in Vincent van Gogh's letters,
in the New Testament Apocrypha,
and in diaries and essays
other people left behind.
They were not complete texts
but sentences, thoughts
Annie put together,
felt, arranged into her life.

She spoke with their voices
because she gathers life
like wildflowers, at random,
mixing colors and scents, distilling
from a homeopathic heart
a remedy for souls gone stale.

Isn't that what morning does?